Football

Julie Murray

Abdo
SPORTS HOW TO
Kids

abdopublishing.com

Published by Abdo Kids, a division of ABDO, PO Box 398166, Minneapolis, Minnesota 55439.

Printed in China

102017

012018

Photo Credits: Glow Images, iStock, Shutterstock, ©The U.S. Navy p.11, ©User: Patrick p.22 / CC-BY-SA 2.0, ©Michael Barera p.22 / CC-BY-SA-4.0

Production Contributors: Teddy Borth, Jennie Forsberg, Grace Hansen

Design Contributors: Christina Doffing, Candice Keimig, Dorothy Toth

Publisher's Cataloging-in-Publication Data

Names: Murray, Julie, author.

Title: Football / by Julie Murray.

Description: Minneapolis, Minnesota : Abdo Kids, 2018. | Series: Sports how to |
Includes glossary, index and online resource (page 24).

Identifiers: LCCN 2017908185 | ISBN 9781532104138 (lib.bdg.) | ISBN 9781532105258 (ebook) |
ISBN 9781532105814 (Read-to-me ebook)

Subjects: LCSH: Football--Juvenile literature. | Football--Terminology--Juvenile literature.

Classification: DDC 796.332 --dc23

LC record available at https://lccn.loc.gov/2017908185

Table of Contents

Football

Joe loves football! He is ready to play.

helmet
pads
jersey
football

Football is played on a field.

Each team has 11 players.

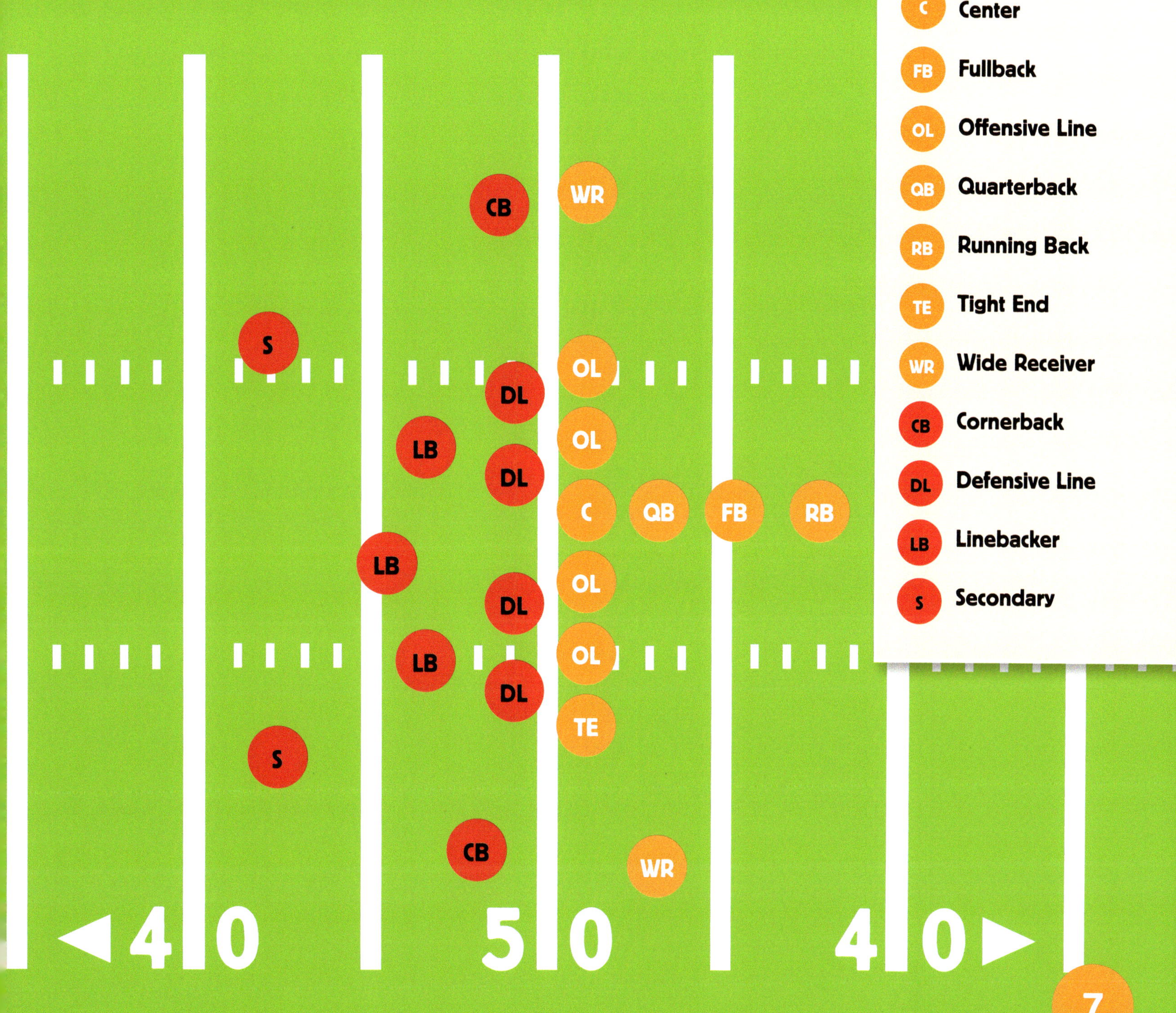

C Center
FB Fullback
OL Offensive Line
QB Quarterback
RB Running Back
TE Tight End
WR Wide Receiver
CB Cornerback
DL Defensive Line
LB Linebacker
S Secondary
CB
WR
S
OL
DL
LB
OL
DL
C
QB
FB
RB
LB
OL
DL
LB
OL
DL
TE
S
CB
WR
40
50
40

An **NFL** game has 4 quarters.

Each one is 15 minutes.

Gillette
STADIUM
VISA
NEW ENGLAND
PATRIOTS
COWBOYS 3
Patriots

The goal is to get to the **end zone**. One team has the ball. They want to move at least 10 yards. They have 4 chances.

Terps
NAVY
Terps

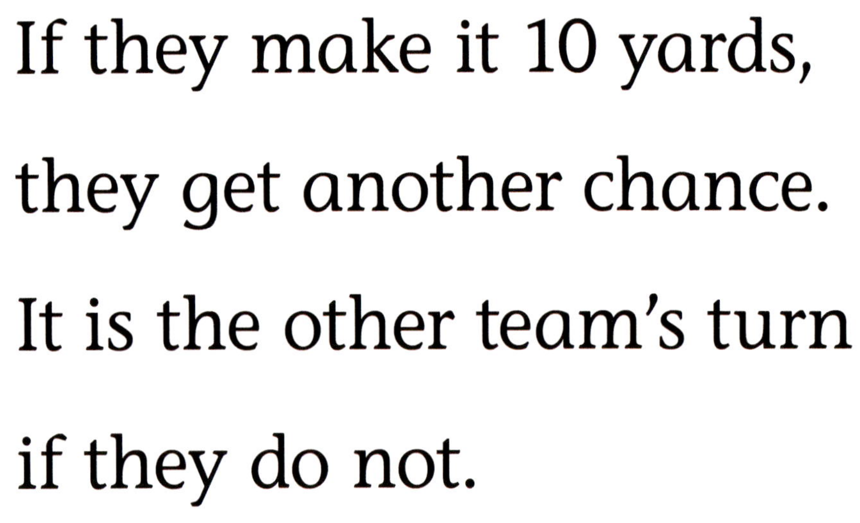

If they make it 10 yards,
they get another chance.
It is the other team's turn
if they do not.

The **quarterback** calls a play. He throws the ball. Lou catches it. First down!

The **defense** tries to stop the ball. Amir makes a tackle.

schutt

Joe runs the ball. Touchdown!

Six points.

Tim kicks the extra point.

They win the game!

KRAFT
Maxwell House

Ways to Score

touchdown: 6 points

extra 1 or 2 points after a touchdown

field goal: 3 points

safety: 2 points

Glossary

defense
the players of a team who try to stop the other team's offense from scoring.

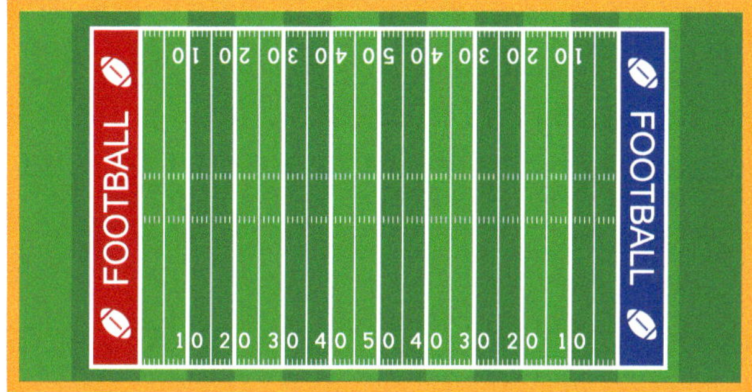

end zone
an area at each end of a football field where the ball must be carried to make a touchdown.

NFL
(National Football League) a major professional American football organization made up of 32 teams.

quarterback
a player who directs a team's offense.

Index

Visit abdokids.com and use this code to access crafts, games, videos, and more!